JOHN THOMPSON'S
EASIEST PIANO COURSE

FIRST DISNEY SONGS

ISBN 978-1-61774-179-1

WILLIS MUSIC

EXCLUSIVELY DISTRIBUTED BY

HAL•LEONARD®
CORPORATION
7777 W. BLUEMOUND RD. P.O. BOX 13819
MILWAUKEE, WISCONSIN 53213

Visit Hal Leonard Online at
www.halleonard.com

Teachers and Parents

This collection of popular Disney songs, arranged in the John Thompson tradition, is intended as supplementary material for the elementary level pianist. The pieces may also be used for sight-reading practice by more advanced students.

CONTENTS

Les Poissons

from Walt Disney's THE LITTLE MERMAID

Music by Alan Menken
Lyrics by Howard Ashman
Arranged by Carolyn Miller

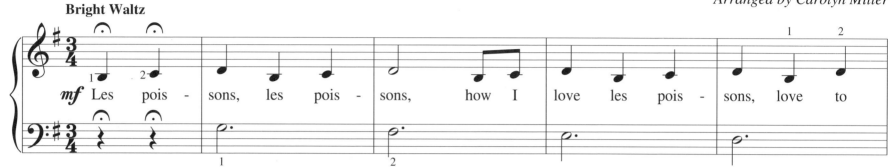

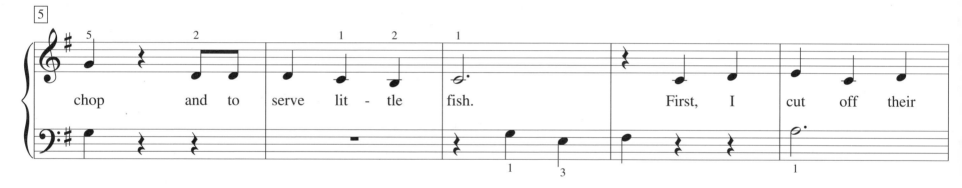

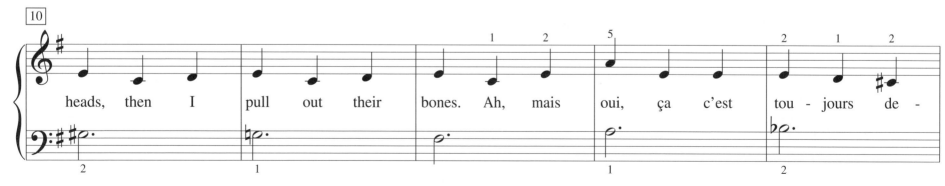

5

Hakuna Matata

from Walt Disney Pictures' THE LION KING

Music by Elton John
Lyrics by Tim Rice
Arranged by Carolyn Miller

wor - ries   for   the   rest   of   your   days. _____   It's   our

prob - lem - free _____   phi - los - o - phy. __   Ha - ku - na ma -

ta - ta! __

Lavender Blue

(Dilly Dilly)
from Walt Disney's SO DEAR TO MY HEART

Words by Larry Morey
Music by Eliot Daniel
Arranged by Carolyn Miller

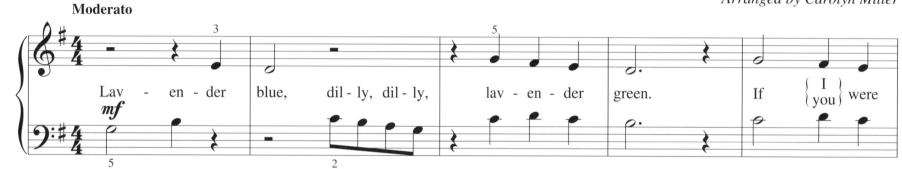

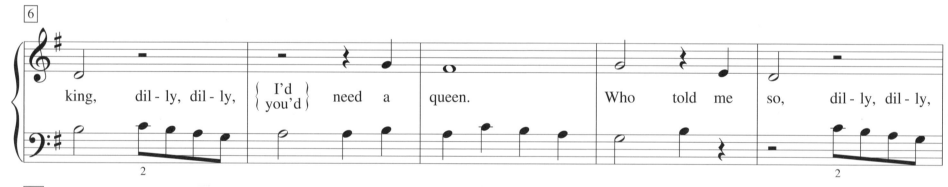

Reflection

from Walt Disney Pictures' MULAN

Music by Matthew Wilder
Lyrics by David Zippel
Arranged by Carolyn Miller

Gently, with expression

Look at me, you may think you see who I real-ly am, but you'll nev-er know me.

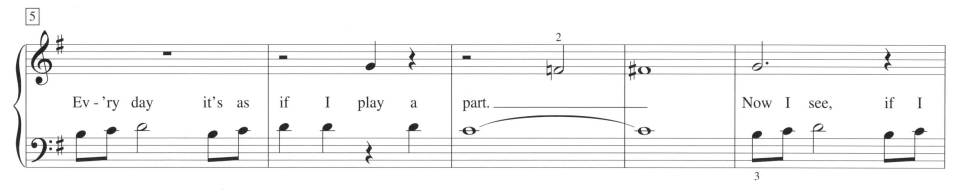

Ev-'ry day it's as if I play a part. Now I see, if I

wear a mask, I can fool the world, but I can-not fool my __ heart. *cresc.*

Chim Chim Cher-ee

from Walt Disney's MARY POPPINS

Words and Music by Richard M. Sherman
and Robert B. Sherman
Arranged by Carolyn Miller

Chim chim-in-ey, chim chim-in-ey, chim chim ___ cher-ee! A sweep is as luck-y as luck-y can be. Chim chim-in-ey, chim chim-in-ey,

You Can Fly! You Can Fly! You Can Fly!

from Walt Disney's PETER PAN

Words by Sammy Cahn
Music by Sammy Fain
Arranged by Carolyn Miller

Friend Like Me

from Walt Disney's ALADDIN

Lyrics by Howard Ashman
Music by Alan Menken
Arranged by Carolyn Miller

Beauty and the Beast
from Walt Disney's BEAUTY AND THE BEAST

Lyrics by Howard Ashman
Music by Alan Menken
Arranged by Carolyn Miller

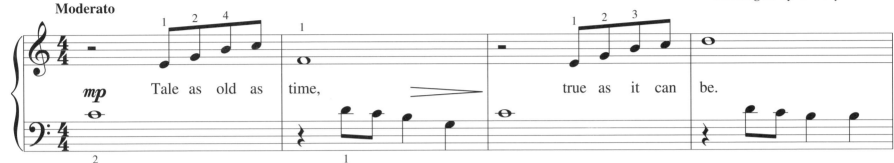

Tale as old as time, true as it can be.

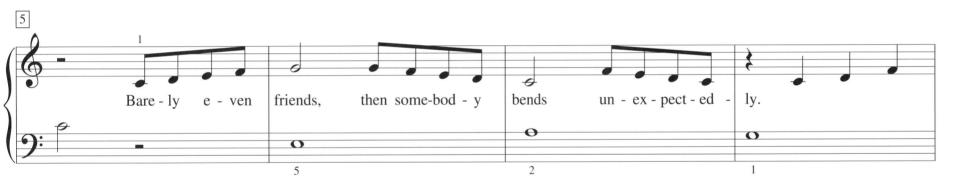

Bare-ly e-ven friends, then some-bod-y bends un-ex-pect-ed-ly.

Just a lit-tle change, small, to say the least. Both a lit-tle

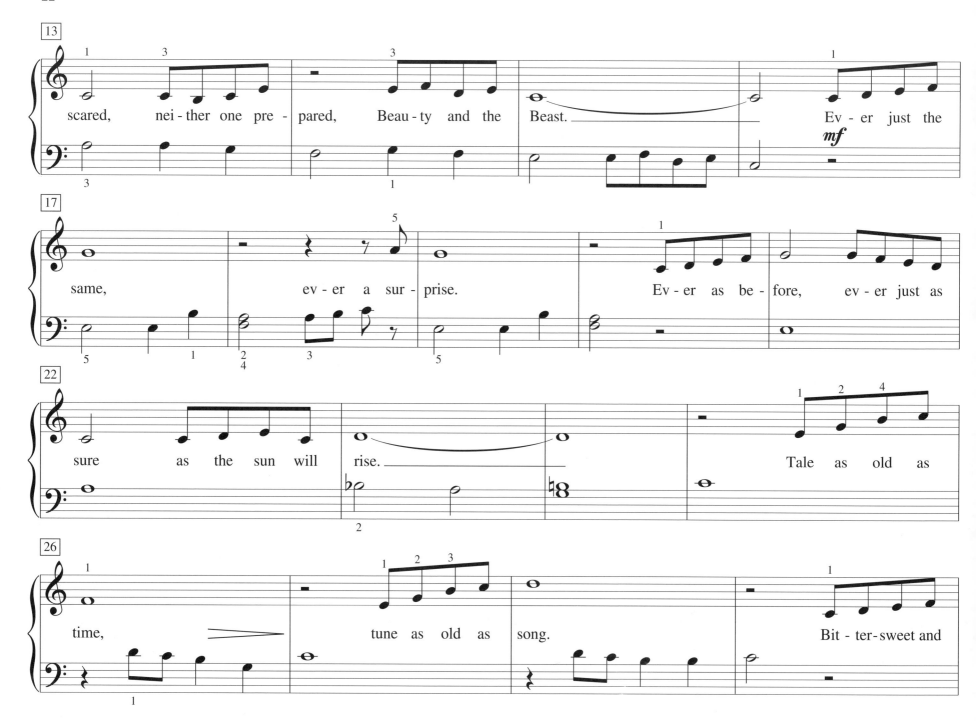

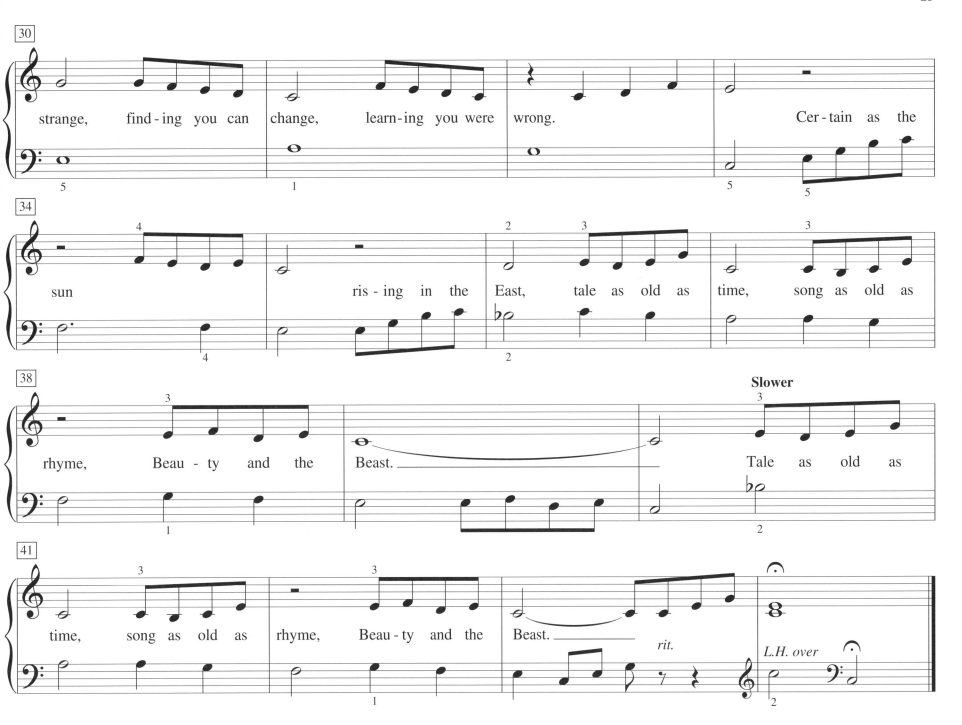

EASIEST PIANO COURSE
Supplementary Songbooks

Fun repertoire books are available as an integral part of **John Thompson's Easiest Piano Course**. Graded to work alongside the course, these pieces are ideal for pupils reaching the end of Part 2. They are invaluable for securing basic technique as well as developing musicality and enjoyment.

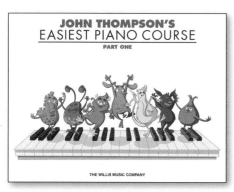

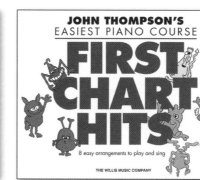

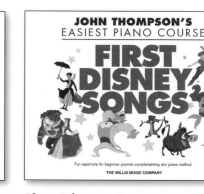

John Thompson's Easiest Piano Course

00414014 Part 1 – Book only $6.99
00414018 Part 2 – Book only $6.99
00414019 Part 3 – Book only $7.99
00414112 Part 4 – Book only $7.99

First Beethoven *arr. Hussey*
00171709 .... $7.99

First Chart Hits – 2nd Edition
00289560 .... $9.99

First Disney Songs *arr. Miller*
00416880 .... $9.99

Also available:

First Children's Songs *arr. Hussey*
00282895 .... $7.99

First Classics
00406347 .... $6.99

First Disney Favorites *arr. Hussey*
00319587 .... $9.99

First Mozart *arr. Hussey*
00171851 .... $7.99

First Nursery Rhymes
00406229 .... $6.99

First Worship Songs *arr. Austin*
00416892 .... $8.99

First Jazz Tunes *arr. Baumgartner*
00120872 .... $7.99

First Pop Songs *arr. Miller*
00416954 .... $8.99

First Showtunes *arr. Hussey*
00282907 .... $9.99

WILLIS MUSIC

EXCLUSIVELY DISTRIBUTED BY
HAL•LEONARD®

Prices, contents and availability subject to change without notice.   Disney Characters and Artwork TM & © 2019 Disney   View complete songlists and more songbooks on **www.halleonard.com**